# Mission, Vision & Pedagogy

Valorie Tatum

www.WeAreAPS.com

Copyright © 2018 by
Valorie Tatum

All rights reserved.
No portion of this book may be reproduced mechanically, electronically, or by any other means, including photocopying, without written permission of the publisher.

ISBN: 978-1-945145-38-4

# **FOREWORD**

The time has come to discover the connections between your mission, vision and pedagogy for life. While reading, keep these questions in mind:

How are you defining the summary of the aims and values of a job, outreach goals and spiritual outcomes for the future?

How will the discipline that deals in and intertwines with various theories and practices redefine the mission, vision and pedagogy circle of life?

How do you determine whether the similarities are strategies that cross all three entities?

How do you employ your judgments and decisions of all three entities with your interactions and understanding to meet the needs of those you encounter?

I have clearly defined what each entity means by standard dictionary definitions: Mission is developed to "meet the need of an individual or collective to carry out the humanitarian work of that individual and/or organization". Vision is "the faculty or state of being able to see. The experience of seeing someone or something in a dream or trans, or as a supernatural apparition". Pedagogy is "the discipline that deals with the theory and practice of teaching". Pedagogy informs teaching strategies, teacher actions, judgements and decisions by taking into consideration theories of learning, understanding of students and their needs, and the backgrounds and interests of individual exposed to the learning outcomes being taught.

# TABLE OF CONTENTS

Mission..................................................page 7
Vision...................................................page 17
Pedagogy..............................................page 27
What I Know.........................................page 35
The Ecumenical Church..........................page 43
Mission, Vision and Pedagogy................page 51
Motivation.............................................page 59
Implementation......................................page 75
Now You Know.....................................page 87
Epilogue................................................page 99

# **Chapter 1: MISSION**

The need to meet the individual or collective to carry out the humanitarian work of that individual and/or organization. The focus must be on my mission as the individual and not the collective, but there must be a concern on whether my mission will adapt to the collective.

I do believe in my mission to commit to the vows that relate to the calling to serve as a United Methodist, who are committed to be loyal to Christ through the resources of the Church and do all in their power to strengthen its ministries. We each have our own identified mission in which each church can clearly see themselves accomplishing the mission to serve the people and God in a manner that goes far beyond than just human feelings.

The Englewood-Rust United Methodist Church's Mission is to demonstrate our love of God and ourselves and to glorify God by reaching out to the community through the gospel, our actions and our ministries. Our domination has a book of discipline in which the language provides an important clarification and it should be used as it forms a strong declaration to support the success of the calling and the outreach work.

**Take a moment to reflect on your mission in life: Personally; Professionally; and Spiritually**

## **Chapter 2: VISION**

Vision is the faculty or state of being able to see; the experience of seeing someone or something in a dream or trance, or as a supernatural apparition. The Vision of Englewood Rust United Methodist Church is as follows: We believe as compassionate Christians that we are empowered to reach beyond our walls to minister to the holistic needs of our community.

Does this vision fit the calling? Yes, it is clearly understanding that the concept is far beyond our actions and will depend on the supernatural powers of God to integrate the necessary resources to reach beyond the church walls. We are used to meet the need of the community no matter the program/ministry implemented.

Making a bold statement puts the deal of covenant into place and a foundation that identifies us with the people and their way of life, which can be risky to implement.

**Can this part of taking and analyzing the mission and vision differ or be more alike than previously noted?**

## Chapter 3: PEDAGOGY

Pedagogy is related to teaching implementation of strategies, results, data and growth. We will begin talking about how pedagogy, in the past has greatly been applied to teaching and/or teachers (with no implied disrespect to the profession). It has taken on negative and unattractive tones, often meaning a dull or overly formal person mainly referencing the teacher or teaching career. So, how does this apply to the mission, and vision? Or does it?

The mission supports and impacts our covenant with God and ourselves. Vision supports and impacts our covenant with God, ourselves, and the community. Pedagogy supports our concepts of the mission and vision to be carried out with the resources that clearly identify the spiritual, learning capacity and sustainable resources to increase the community needs being met especially where they live. So, the concept of teaching is not that far from the church and its beliefs. We are teaching the community to locate and utilize resources to meet the following needs (food, clothing, housing, education).

**What are some of the resources that you can utilize in your community?**

## Chapter 4: WHAT I KNOW

Stated in *Our Membership Vows in The United Methodist Church*, by Mark W. Stamm: "The body and blood of Christ, which (according to the Scriptures) makes individuals a part of the church (1Corinthians 11:23-12:30)". We call these children "baptized members". Granted, we do not yet call them professing members, as that title is reserved for persons who exercise governance in the church and are expected to carry out its various ministries. Nevertheless, we insist that these children are already part of God's covenant family. Such status is "God's gift" and we insist is, "offered to us without price".

However, if the individual vows (mission, vision, pedagogy) are implemented and kept, the person carrying out the church's mission, vision and pedagogy will be nurtured, raised up and reaching the masses of the church and community life. Thus, the individual must be part of the key components where they will learn the biblical language, engage in prayer, develop relationships with the community that promote collaboration, and welcome protocol in the church. This is how and where mission, vision, and pedagogy overlap.

**If Jesus ate with and educated the poor and gave them eternal life, is it possible to consistently sustain the people to build and follow through. How?**

# Chapter 5: THE ECUMENICAL CHURCH ON MISSION, VISION AND PEDAGOGY

Do the three entities hold a sin factor? Yes, when people, both individuals as well as small and large groups, are given certain spiritual powers and commissions (these are often found in leadership positions), we risk falling into two problems: sin and evil. The statement may sound judgmental, primitive and one-sided. However, the church on many occasions and in consensus, insists that renouncing sin and evil is a foundational part to move in the mission, vision and pedagogy of the church and one's ministry in the church/community life.

How does the mission, vision and pedagogy work in the church? Are our ways different from what those outside the church may do? When communities need support, do they follow the process of identifying the mission, vision and pedagogy to reach the needs and wants of the masses in a respective area? Do we know why the sin factor is very real, and moving constantly throughout the church in its endeavors to meet the needs of the mission, vision and pedagogy goals of the church and the person implementing them?

My grandmother recalled when the elders would say, "Sin can be conscious or unconscious, depending on the individual involved. It, at times, is done to meet a need that an individual is lacking; it is an immoral act considered to be a transgression against divine law in God eyes". She stated that the person may be more apt to recovery through forgiveness and grace in comparison to evil, which is clearly defined as profound immorality, wickedness and depravity especially when regarded as a supernatural force. This requires the use of great force both spiritually (intercessory prayers and baptism) and naturally.

**Do we know why the evil factor is at times not connected with the sin factor and why they are perceived as being different entities?**

# Chapter 6: MISSION, VISION AND PEDAGOGY TODAY

We have discussed the clear confusion of the three entities, but what is the motivation for the involvement of the three existing in our lives? Has my life been transformed by the Gospel utilizing these three key elements? In our early learning, whether Sunday School or Bible School, the very reasons these three elements exist is clear. They are grounded in the character of God, the establishing of the command of Christ, and the deepening compulsion of the role of the Holy Spirit. They foster the need for the lost and nurture those who have never heard of the Gospel.

To understand the background stage and theology of these elements, let's take a look at the Character of God, the Command of Christ, the compulsion of the Holy Spirit and the Condition of the Lost. I will be utilizing points and arguments from the World Missions Today (What You Should Know About Global Ministries) Evangelical Training Association.

# What is your perspective on the character of God?

# Chapter 7: MOTIVATION FOR MISSION, VISION AND PEDAGOGY

*The Character of God*

We know God is holy and hates sin. He is the author and owner of eternal punishment for Satan and his angels that rebelled against God in the beginning and end. We know that we are made in his image but suffer with the same rebellious nature as Satan, but it is not his goal to see us perish with Satan.

The one thing God gave us that he did not give Satan is salvation through Jesus Christ his beloved son. The requirement is that we must know, hear and believe the Gospel. If we are not aware of this we will receive judgement from God in which they deserve, because he is a holy God he cannot accept sinners until they are redeemed and clearly the mission, vision and pedagogy is based on both his holiness and his love to be effective and sustainable for life in the kingdom.

*The Command of Christ*

It is clearly without doubt Jesus involved every believer in missions, carrying out the vision and engaging through teachable pedagogy. This does not mean, however, that every woman, man and child are compelled to be missionaries, but there are those who will lead others and instruct them in the way of being disciples and disciplined in the word.

Jesus made very clear during his last supper, the Passover discussion and the resurrection night that command has a universal application. The application is obedience and it is not optional. Jesus reminded his disciples and us, "If you love Me, you will keep My commandments" (John 14:15). Who are we that we will follow this to work within our mission, vision and pedagogy to his people and meeting the outward/outreach needs.

*The Compulsion of the Holy Spirit*

It has been more than 2000 years since early Christians did not appeal to the Great commission to fuel their compassion for lost souls/persons. It was noted it flowed from their encounter with the Spirit of the Living God and their inward compulsion to share with others what they experienced, witnessed and was in awe of.

Today, we are not sure if miracles and signs still exist according to God. We have such a spirit of instant gratification that we seek to make it happen for ourselves or through others. Trusting others to be the implementers of our happiness, giving away our free choice. "For we cannot but speak the things we have seen and heard, exclaimed Peter and John to those who sought to silence them" (Acts 4:20). What happened to opening up to the Holy Spirit and communicating with God to release power in us and around us.

*The Condition of the Lost*

We often pray for the sick, shut in, homeless, heretics, unbelievers, mourners and already deceased are these the lost and what do we understand about their condition? Is it too late for the lost? In Luke 16:23-28, the rich man in Hades cried out for mercy and asked that Lazarus the beggar be sent with a drop of water to cool his tongue. He was told it was too late, he begged that someone be sent to warn his five brothers.

This has been noted as no more of an eloquent appeal for missions, visions and pedagogy has ever been uttered and I must agree. This is a prime and compelling reason for mission, vision and pedagogy to be evident in the church and in the Christian life especially for this world.

The separation and judgement of God is forth coming and irreversible. If we are not implementing these three elements billions will sit in darkness without revelation of the light and eternal salvation. Three elements are in essential and urgent need for the lost man, woman and child.

# How do you feel that sin effects your life?

## Chapter 8: RESULTS OF IMPLEMENTATION

The stage setting for implementing mission, vision and pedagogy in your Christian life and church is often the source for the growth of a church. The implementation of the three elements help churches to define church beliefs governing the lost. The three elements help churches to clearly identify resources to support local and worldwide outreach ministries. The three elements elevate the roles and values for believers being spiritually healthy.

So, going back to the beginning how does it all wrap around my life to move forward in my role in the church and my spiritual outcomes. Clearly, the three do overlap and provide the foundation for my goals to develop strong programing in my church to reach the lost by developing my knowledge of doctrine dealing with the authority of Scripture, the hopeless conditions of the lost and the necessity for faith in Christ for salvation. It is vital to build up areas in prayer, church and family, and financial gifts so that the church is equipped to maintain itself in capacity and sustainable areas.

**What ways can you improve your prayer life? Church? Family? Finances?**

IMPLEMENTATION

IMPLEMENTATION

# Chapter 9: NOW YOU KNOW THE PLAN OF MISSIONS, VISIONS AND PEDAGOGIES

The three elements promote the happiness of people engulfed in the greatness of God. This is true only if the people know God; we want all we do and know to be useful with humility for edification of the kingdom. People must know God. They cannot delight in God if they don't know him. They will fall prey to false Gods and prophets, which in itself is deeply disturbing.

I am a teacher of academics (reading, writing, math, science and social studies). This doesn't mean God's greatness should not be revealed to my students. When we nurture, model and set consequences, we are teaching them how to be disciples. Utilizing these skills even in a corporate world will bring about a disciple who loves his brethren, evidence or right relationships, attracting others resulting in a multiplication of converts. "And he gave some...to be pastors and teachers, for the perfecting of the saints for the work of the ministry, for the edifying of the body of Christ" (Eph. 4:11-13, NKJV). When the body of Christ utilizes their gifts, the body will function in spiritual maturity, missions, visions and pedagogies will result in growing disciples for the kingdom.

# How can you use your gift(s) to help edify others?

## **EPILOGUE**

The time I wrote this book has given me the clarity to move into my next levels in my church and spiritual life. I have applied to seminary school in which I will be focusing on African American Ministries and Black Church Studies Certificated Programs to support my community and my goals later towards becoming a deaconess, with the will of God and his guidance, Amen.

www.ingramcontent.com/pod-product-compliance
Lightning Source LLC
Chambersburg PA
CBHW061456040426
42450CB00008B/1385